THE GHOSTLY TALES OF COLORADO'S FRONT RANGE

Colorado

Wyoming

- 🪦1 Fort Collins
- 🪦1 Greeley
- 🪦2 Longmont
- 🪦1 Fort Lupton
- 🪦3 Boulder
- 🪦2 Louisville
- 🪦3 Golden
- 🪦4 Denver
- 🪦5 Littleton
- 🪦5 Castle Rock
- 🪦5 Leadville
- 🪦6 Larkspur
- 🪦7 Colorado Springs
- 🪦7 Pueblo

New Mexico ↓

NEBRASKA

Table of Contents & Map Key

Introduction 3
1. Chapter 1. Fort Collins 7
2. Chapter 2. Longmont 23
3. Chapter 3. Boulder 33
4. Chapter 4. Denver 45
5. Chapter 5. Leadville 65
6. Chapter 6. Larkspur 83
7. Chapter 7. Colorado Springs .93

KANSAS

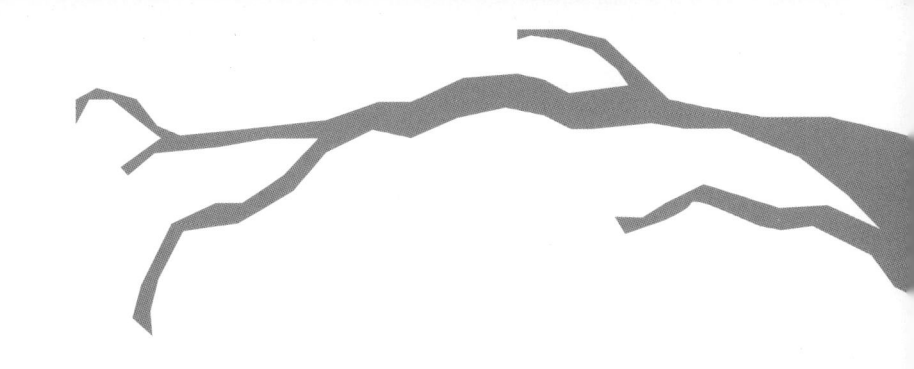

Introduction

In 1876, Colorado became the thirty-eighth state of the United States of America, and its official nickname became the "Centennial State." "Centennial" refers to a one-hundredth anniversary, and Colorado officially became a state one-hundred years after the signing of the Declaration of Independence in 1776. It is also called "Colorful Colorado," and this one is easy to figure out. All you have to do is take a quick look around at the beautiful flowers, trees, rivers, and mountains, and you'll understand immediately what inspired this nickname.

There's a lot to see and do in Colorado, from skiing and rock climbing, to touring old mines and panning for gold. Colorado has four national parks, including Rocky Mountain National Park, home to Long's Peak, the highest peak in the Front Range, at 14,259 feet. The parks are full of amazing wildlife, and you may spot elk, moose, bighorn sheep, and even a bear or two!

The Front Range is a two-hundred-mile section of the Rocky Mountains that divides Colorado almost down the middle. It is sometimes called the "backbone." This area stretches from the Arkansas River in southern Colorado north to the Wyoming border. The towns located along the mountains and foothills of the Front Range are called the Front

INTRODUCTION

Range Urban Corridor. These towns, including Boulder, Golden, Denver, and Colorado Springs, are also home to a variety of wildlife. And in certain places, there is a chance you might spot more than elk, moose, sheep, or even bears—you might see ghosts!

You could catch a glimpse of a shadow sneaking around the corner or feel a set of eyes staring at you in the dark. You could even encounter a mysterious image in plain sight, one that doesn't try to hide at all. It might be a mischief maker, but then again, it could be a much calmer spirit.

We'll be traveling north to south on our Front Range ghost tour, so get ready. Here we go!

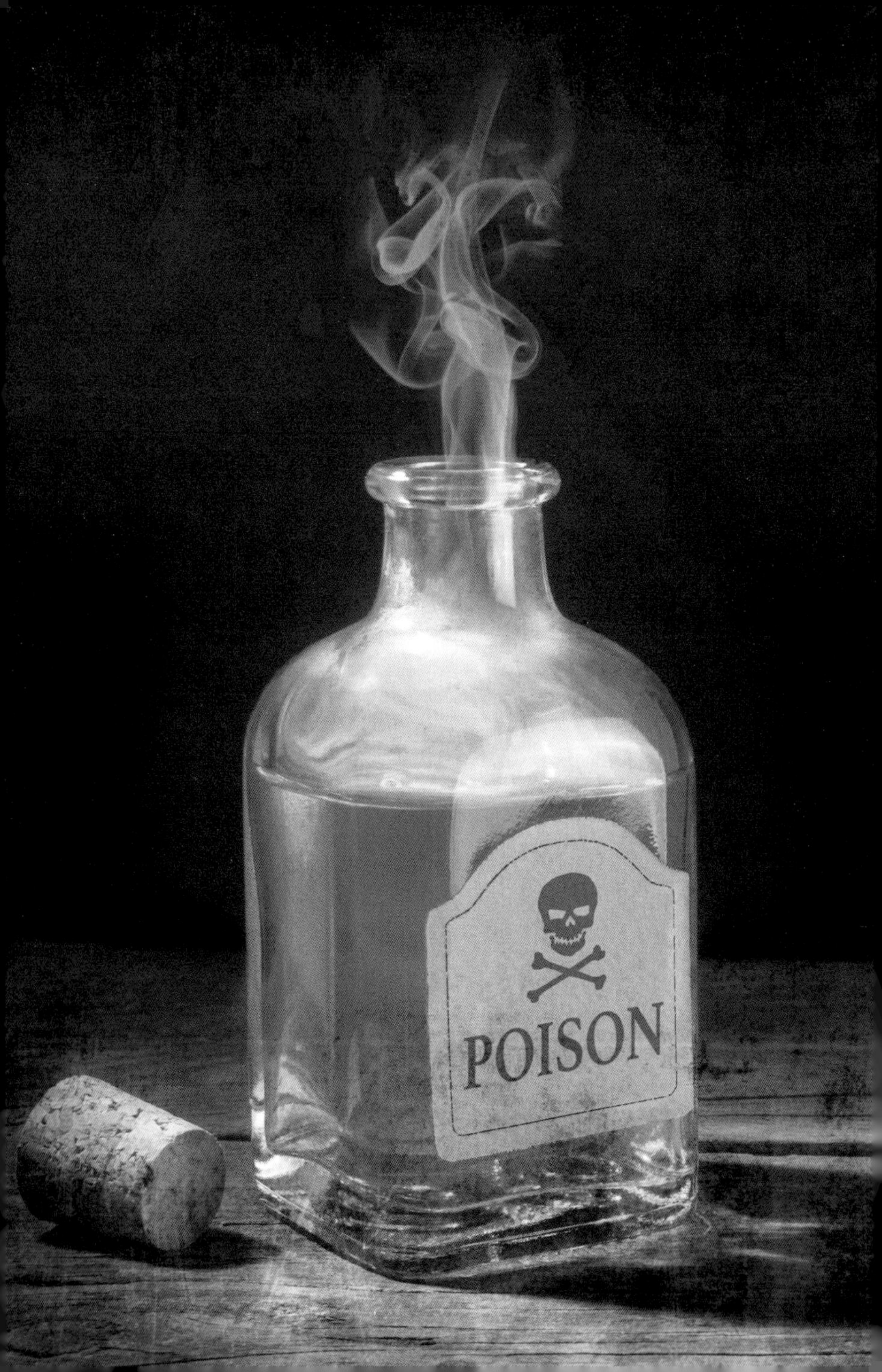
POISON

CHAPTER 1

Fort Collins

Northern Colorado was not a very busy place in the nineteenth century. The area now known as Fort Collins saw only a few stagecoaches and trains traveling along the roads and tracks. Fur trappers and travelers passed through now and again but, overall, it was pretty quiet. Then along came the gold rush, and things were never so quiet again.

Camp Collins, which would later become Fort Collins, was established in 1862. It was a military fort named for Lieutenant Colonel William Collins. The fort was little more than a cluster of cabins and tents on the banks of the Poudre River. In 1867, this military fort was closed and abandoned, leaving behind a small military cemetery.

By 1910, an actual town was taking shape, and the Fort Collins military cemetery ground was planned to be the site of the Fort Collins Post Office. The graves had no markers, and only six bodies were found and relocated before construction of the post office began. Other bodies likely still remain in their original graves, possibly now under buildings or sidewalks.

Fort Collins today is a busy city. It is home to Colorado State University, many tech companies, restaurants, and nearly 170,000 people. That's the count for living people, anyway. No one is sure how many ghosts are there, but a few of them are pretty well known. And like anyone else, ghosts have their favorite spots.

STARBUCKS
(172 North College)

Imagine you are an exhausted Colorado State University student who has been hunched over a Starbucks table, studying for hours. You have a big test tomorrow, and you still have a lot more studying to do, but you realize you can't read another paragraph without stretching your legs and drinking some more coffee or tea (or smartly remembering to rehydrate with water). Maybe you'll buy a snack to go with your drink, too.

Your legs feel stiff from being tucked under the table for so long while you were sitting, but you're about to have plenty of time to straighten them out. The line is long. Everyone waiting in front of you looks super tired, too. You are all basically dressed the same: sweats, T-shirts, and whatever comfortable shoes you could slip your feet into on your way out the door.

As you yawn for the hundredth time, you catch someone moving forward from the corner of your eye. Wait! Is she trying to cut the line? Who does she think she is? Then your eyes focus, and you really see her. Whoa!

Where did she come from? This woman sure isn't dressed like a typical college student. She is dressed in Victorian-style clothing—long heavy dress, lace-up boots, and a hat that looks like a bird crash-landed into a pile of ribbons on her head.

At first, you figure she probably just finished performing in a play or has a part in one of the local tourist attractions. But when you take a longer look, she doesn't appear as solid as everyone else. And her boots, they're . . . um, not exactly touching the floor? What the holy iced-mocha is happening here? Why is no one else staring? Are you the only one who sees her? Okay, maybe you should've taken a break much sooner.

But what if your eyes aren't playing tricks on you? What if she's really there? Could she be a ghost? A ghost who drinks coffee? A modern coffee shop would certainly be interesting for someone from Victorian times. You wonder what fascinates her more: the silver whipped cream canisters, the blenders, or the microwaves. Maybe the paper cups? They didn't have those in Victorian times either. Does she even know what a Frappuccino even is?

If only you didn't have so much studying left to do, you could offer to share your table with her and ask her all these questions and more. WHAT are you thinking? You can't chat over a cup of coffee with a ghost! Or ... can you?

It might not be the last time you see her.

This Victorian lady is actually a regular at this Starbucks location. She may step in front of you again someday. You probably won't try to stop her then either, but she'll be gone before you even get up the nerve to ask her anything.

Beau Jo's Pizza in the Avery Building
(Corner Of Mountain Avenue And College Avenue)

The Avery Building was constructed by William Avery in 1901, who supposedly died after "accidentally" swallowing a fatal dose of arsenic. That's what his wife said, anyway. Some people in town didn't believe it was an accident. After all, his wife married his business partner only twelve days later. That does seem kind of quick, right? No wonder people were suspicious that she might have been covering up her murderous deed. But a trial found the widow and her new husband not guilty, so

William Avery's official cause of death remains an "accidental" poisoning.

What do you think William Avery would've said if he'd had a chance to speak at that trial? Would he have confirmed his wife was innocent or called her out as a murderer? Unfortunately, he never got the chance to tell his side of the story. He was a little too dead to speak up for himself. But what if he has found another way to communicate since then?

Well, in Beau Jo's pizza shop—in the building that bears Avery's name—there's an entity who shoves forks and spoons around on customers' tables. Some say that's William Avery himself! Maybe he's trying to warn everyone to pay closer attention to what goes into their mouths. He probably wishes someone had warned him.

FORT LUPTON

In 1837, Lancaster Lupton established the fort in his name and became a fur trader. (In case you're wondering, the "fort' was actually a trading post.) Lupton had a bit of a bad reputation. He had been a lieutenant in the military until he quickly resigned to avoid being punished for fighting. And he didn't exactly have the best head for business, either.

At one point, he owned Fort Lupton and a second fort in Wyoming. His forts were known for nonstop parties that often resulted in loud fights with plenty of shouting. It wasn't uncommon for shots to be fired. His forts were definitely not places to get a good night's rest. Lupton wasn't able to keep both forts in business for long. He sold his Wyoming fort in 1842, and Fort Lupton shut down in 1844 when the fur trade declined, just seven short years after it was founded.

Over the years, the original Fort Lupton structure crumbled. Everything except one wall and the original bricks had deteriorated. Thankfully, in 2008, the South Platte Historical Society reconstructed the building, and it can be visited now close to its original site. Current residents of the town of Fort Lupton have preserved many of the other old homes and buildings in the area. And it seems some of the previous owners might not be impressed with their efforts.

The St. John Building
(410 Denver Avenue, Fort Lupton)

The St. John Building was constructed by Edgar St. John more than a century ago, in 1912. He built it to be a mercantile, or general store. In 2007, an Italian restaurant named Wholly

Stromboli moved into the space, and in 2010, the owners began some renovations and repairs. And that's when things got weird.

Staff members and visitors reported being touched by someone they couldn't see, and they heard voices that also had no bodies attached to them. Forks started flying off tables, and pots and pans flew off shelves in the kitchen.

A team of paranormal investigators recorded more than ten electronic voice phenomena, or EVPs. EVPs are sounds that are recorded by paranormal experts and investigators on special equipment. These recordings are claimed to be the voices of spirits who are trying to communicate with the living world. When the investigators asked if there were any spirits present who wished to speak with them, one voice said, "I would." An investigator saw a full-bodied shadow of a man cross through the light shaft by the stairwell leading upstairs.

The apparition was so lifelike, he thought it was a crew member at first. Some people believe it was the ghost of Edgar St. John.

But others think the strange activities that occur there are the actions of a different spirit: Edgar's daughter, who died when she was very young. Paranormal investigators believe they also heard her speak and that she may have told them her name. They couldn't be sure, but it sounded like a voice said "Haley" or "Halley" or "Nellie." When they went upstairs, one of the investigators was looking at a picture of the St. John family that was hanging in the bar. She picked it up, and the frame fell apart. Along the bottom of the picture were the names of the family members: Edgar, his son Patrick, his wife Patricia, and their daughter—Nellie.

The staff at Wholly Stromboli has learned to live with the ghosts, but they can't seem to make them behave.

GREELEY

Greeley was originally called "the Union Colony," but it was renamed in 1870 when Horace Greeley, the famous newspaperman who founded the *New York Tribune*, visited the town.

Greeley is best known for its meat-packing industry. (Meat-packing companies process livestock for sale as food products.) Greeley is also known as the agricultural center of the sugar beet industry. At the height of production in the 1920s, Greeley manufactured and supplied nearly one-fourth of all the sugar sold in the entire United States. It was a pretty sweet place!

Like most old towns, Greeley has historic buildings. Those old structures were built to last, and their architecture still impresses local residents and visitors—even those from beyond the grave.

The Weld County Courthouse
(901 Ninth Avenue, Greeley)

The Weld County Courthouse was built with solid materials like granite and marble. In fact, every last bit of building-worthy marble was taken from the quarries in Marble, Colorado, for its construction. This sturdy building is still in use as a courthouse, but some visitors show up for less serious matters.

Johnathan, a little boy ghost who runs around the fourth floor, likes attention and will make himself known by playing with toys or clicking on typewriter keys. The back staircase is another spot he likes. He is a prankster, too, and he doesn't seem to be afraid of heights. A child's handprint has been known to spontaneously appear—on the ceiling! Good trick, Johnathan.

The courthouse staff leaves toys out for him to play with, and they are frequently moved, along with items in the offices. Hey, if you give a kid a toy, of course he's going to play with it. And if they don't want Johnathan messing with other stuff in their office, maybe they should lock the door. On second thought, that might not keep him out. Ghosts don't care about locks.

Johnathan is the only known child spirit in the courthouse, but there are grown-ups haunting the place as well. Adult faces, often frightening ones, appear reflected in the courthouse's eight antique clocks. Adult voices, including a long sigh, and scuffling footsteps are also heard in the courthouse.

The fourth floor was originally used as a space for juries (the people who decide if someone is guilty or innocent in a trial), and it is now one of the busiest areas for spirits. Johnathan isn't alone up there. A tall man in a dark coat can be seen in the hallway walking past the steps. He is thought to be Wilbur "W.D."

French, a rancher suspected of murdering his business partner. It is believed he may still hang out on the fourth floor because he's waiting to hear the jury's decision in his case.

During his lifetime, W.D. French was known to be quick with his gun, and he didn't mind threatening people who stood in his way. Maybe he paces that fourth-floor hallway as a threat to the jurors, sending a message that they better find him not guilty—or else. He doesn't have his gun anymore, but when a murderous ghost shows up, you kind of get the message.

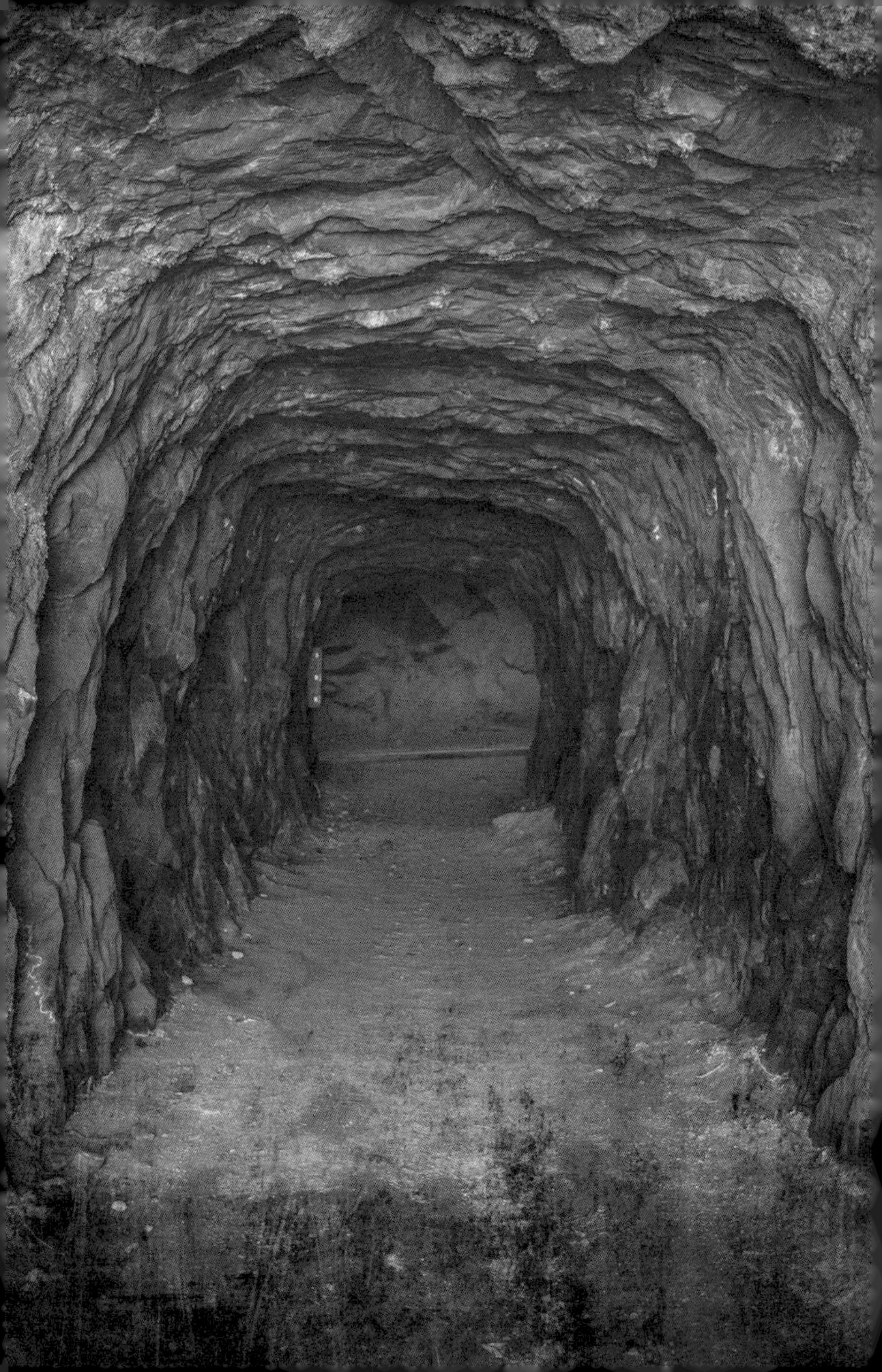

Chapter 2

Longmont

Longmont was founded in 1871 by a group of people from Chicago, Illinois. It was originally called the Chicago-Colorado Colony. The town's current name comes from Longs Peak (the highest point in Rocky Mountain National Park, remember?), which is clearly visible from Longmont, and from the French word for mountain: *montagne*. Longmont certainly has its fair share of ghosts as well.

The Hansen Building
(477 Main Street, Longmont)

The Hanson Building is the former home of Colorado Telephone and Telegraph Company. It is now home to a law firm where the sound of a ringing phone can often be heard, even when the office phones aren't ringing at all. Could these phantom rings be the echoes of the once busy phone company? Maybe a spirit trying to deliver a message? If a ghost called your phone, would you answer?

The Vance Brand Civic Auditorium
(600 East Mountain View, Longmont)

The Vance Brand Civic Auditorium is cared for by a spectral janitor who has been nicknamed Edison because he enjoys tampering with the electrical system. (You know, like Thomas Edison, the American inventor of the incandescent lightbulb.) It is believed this ghostly janitor died when a balcony fell on him. That's really no way for a building to thank its janitor. He must still love the place, though.

Edison's footsteps are often heard on the catwalks, and cold spots have been reported along them. Catwalks are a great place to oversee an auditorium, so it makes sense Edison would be up there. A shadowy figure can also be seen occupying a seat in the audience or moving between the rows. This apparition is believed to be Edison, too. After all the hard work he does, he deserves to take a break now and then. All work and no play could make a ghost ... well, maybe we don't want to find out. Enjoy the show, Edison!

LOUISVILLE

Louisville is a former coal-mining town located right in the middle of Colorado's northern coalfield (an area containing large amounts of underground coal deposits). The first mine there, the Welch Mine, opened in 1877. Louisville officially became a town in 1882.

Although coal mining was a huge part of Louisville's history, little shows of it today, at least above ground. Underground is a different story. Like so many other cities in Colorado, Louisville sits atop a series of tunnels. The tunnels were used to deliver coal to local businesses who used it for heat. Some people believe other things may have been delivered through the tunnels as well, like liquor during a time when it was illegal. But over time, tunnels are known to collapse. There is said to be at least one collapsed shaft under Louisville.

The tunnels run under the town like honeycomb, but the entrances are all sealed off now, and not everyone is happy about that. Some of the local ghosts are very displeased about being denied access to the tunnels, and they don't mind letting everyone know how they feel, especially in local restaurants.

The Melting Pot Restaurant
(732 Main Street, Louisville)

This restaurant is said to have a collapsed shaft from one of the area's many underground tunnels beneath it. Three bootleggers (people who sell something illegally, often liquor) were supposedly killed when a delivery through the tunnels went wrong. The staff at the Melting Pot thinks at least one of the men is still in the restaurant's basement. He's down there, appearing as a ghostly shadow, making strange noises, and removing screws from support beams. Is it just his way of complaining about the botched delivery and trying to find his way out of the tunnel?

Bootleggers were outlaws who lived by their own rules and didn't care about the laws, so the ghost of a bootlegger stuck in a basement must be one seriously frustrated spirit.

Colacci's
(816 Main Street, Louisville)

This restaurant also has a blocked-off tunnel entrance in the basement, and the staff believes they, too, have their own resident ghost down there. They say their basement is home to another bootlegger killed in another delivery gone wrong.

But Colacci's bootlegger ghost is a woman. She lets them know she is not at all happy about being trapped in a basement by smashing light bulbs and chilling the air. When you trap an angry ghost in your basement, what do you expect?

The Old Louisville Inn
(740 Front Street, Louisville)
Note: The Old Louisville Inn has since closed.

This building has loads of charming features, including an 1880s antique bar. The bar has all the expected design details of the time period, plus another original feature: a bullet hole! Coughs and disembodied voices, including that of a spirit known as Samantha, who may have once lived in the building, are often heard.

Voices being heard in a haunted building isn't unusual, but much like that original bar with its unexpected bullet hole, the Old Louisville Inn is home to another unexpected sight on occasion: a disembodied hand at the cash register! A ghostly hand, nothing more—a hand that moves over the keys without the assistance of a body or even an arm.

It might be best to pay with cash at this place. You wouldn't want to have to hand over your credit card to a disembodied hand, would you? To be on the safe side, just drop your money on the bar, and forget about your change.

To be fair, the hand hasn't grabbed anyone yet, but it hasn't promised not to either.

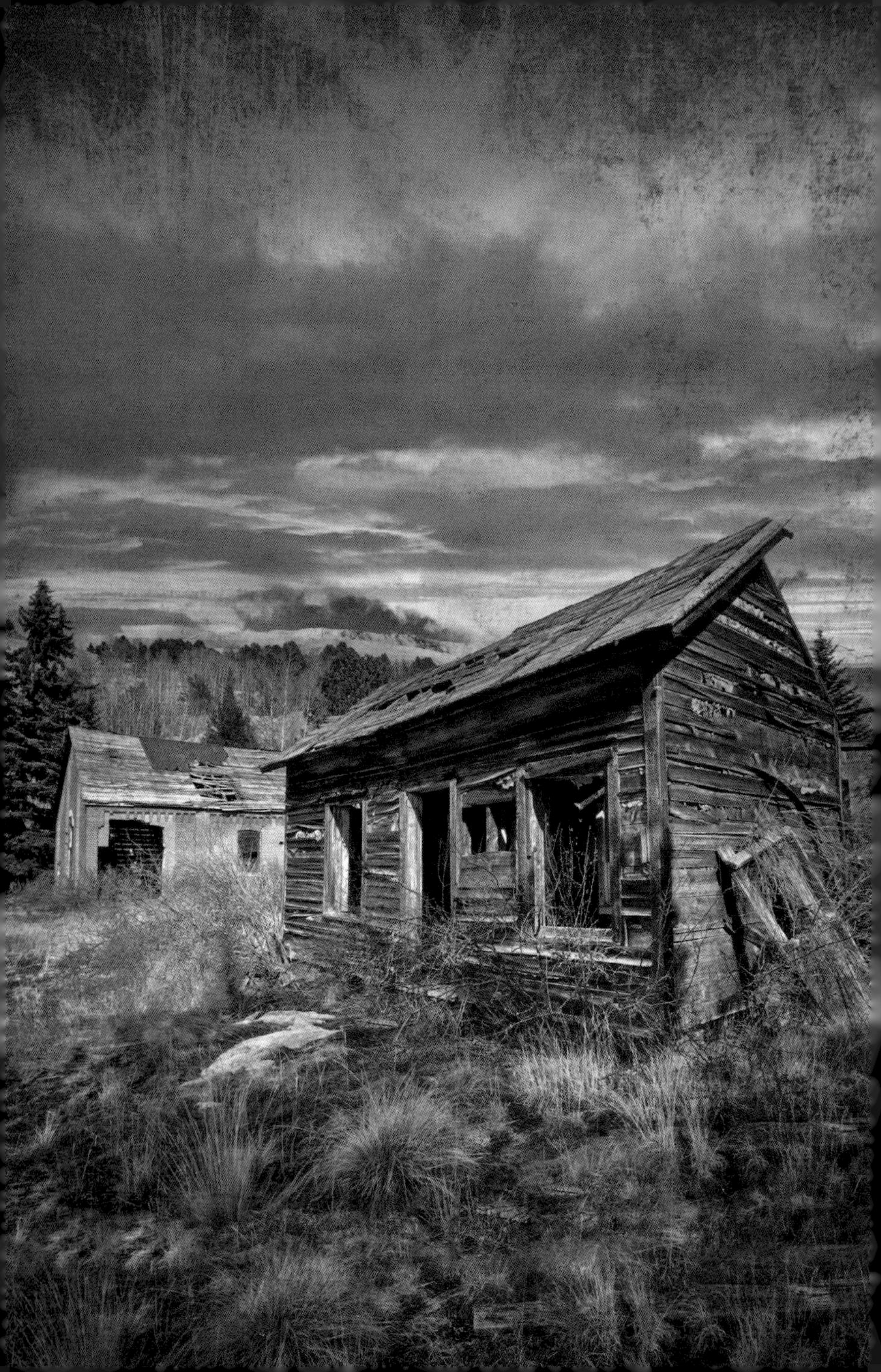

CHAPTER 3

Boulder

Miners in the mountain towns needed a convenient place to buy supplies, and the area in the foothills that is now known as Boulder was the perfect location for them. Boulder City, as it was first known, was officially recognized in 1861 as part of the Nebraska Territory, but it was later transferred to the Colorado Territory. Boulder, Colorado, remains a great shopping destination, although shoppers today come in search of different merchandise than the miners of the 1800s.

Boulder was also home to the first campus of the University of Colorado. The university was founded there in 1876, just five months before Colorado became a state. (Go, Buffaloes!) Any town with a major university will host countless visitors, and Boulder is no exception. Some of those visitors choose to make Boulder their lifelong (and afterlife) home.

Hotel Boulderado
(2115 13th Street, Boulder)

Hotel Boulderado was once a stopping place for miners, ranchers, and the occasional visiting celebrity, but some guests never checked out. A ghost mother carrying her baby has been seen wandering the hallways and stairs. The halls are also where a mysterious white-robed figure can be spotted. The white-robed figure prefers to stay in the upper corridors.

In March 2016, a photo captured a woman with waist-length brown hair on an upper-floor balcony during a wedding reception. But that woman wasn't a wedding guest—she was a ghost! Those newlyweds got quite a special gift on their special day!

It is rumored that if you like staying in haunted hotel rooms, you should check into rooms 302, 304, or 517. You might pass the mother and her crying baby, the white-robed ghost, or some other ghost on the way to your room. Who knows who you might encounter once you close the door and turn out the lights? But don't worry. You'll probably be able to check out whenever you're ready. Probably.

The Pearl Street Mall
(Pearl Street, Boulder)

This popular shopping area contains blocks of stores and restaurants. It's known for unique shops and the many street performers (known as buskers)—fire swallowers, dancers, and college students playing musical instruments—hoping to earn some cash as shoppers make their way along the mall.

One store, El Loro, has its own whimsical character: a spirit the staff calls "the Bird." This entity moves things around and sometimes makes items disappear—only to have them show up again with no logical explanation. El

Loro is home to another being, too. This one stays in the basement and does not give off friendly vibes at all. The basement at El Loro also has a blocked-off tunnel entrance, so this could be another spirit who is unhappy about being trapped for eternity in a mildewy basement.

Out on the mall, a "person" is often seen walking by Ninth Avenue and Pearl Street, the site of an old blacksmith shop and sometimes along Boulder Creek. It is the image of a man wearing a dark hat and looking at the ground. He is believed to be William Tull, who was hanged in Boulder in 1867 for stealing horses. After his arrest, he was held at the blacksmith shop until the time of his hanging.

It was later proven that William Tull had not stolen the horses after all. He had purchased them from his employer. The town had hanged an innocent man. Maybe he is searching for his horses, or maybe he's searching for the men who unjustly executed him.

GOLDEN

Golden is another former supply town. Today, it is best known for Colorado School of Mines, a public research university that has been in existence ever since 1874, and the Coors Brewery. Golden's Washington Street is home to houses, small business, and several interesting shops. It's not a big town, but it has a rich history, and there is much to love about it. Some find it a hard place to leave.

The Rocky Mountain Quilt Museum
(200 Violet Street, Golden)

This quilt museum, which is known as RMQM, was founded by longtime Golden resident

Eugenia Mitchell in 1991. Mitchell donated 101 of her best quilts to start the museum's collection. She died in 2006 at the age of 103. RMQM's first home was upstairs from a Chinese restaurant, and it shared the space with a Navy recruiting office.

One morning, a museum staffer named Kathy was met by the Navy recruiter who told her he had been disturbed by footsteps pacing up and down the hallway the night before. She assured him it was just "Eugenia," checking to make sure her quilts were being taken care of.

The spirit, believed to be Eugenia, continued to make appearances and remained peaceful until the night before the museum was moved in 2017. Kathy came in to find Eugenia's quilts scattered all over the floor. They had been neatly stacked the night before. Nothing else was out of place.

Eugenia might not have liked the idea of the museum being relocated, or perhaps she didn't understand what was happening. Maybe she thought the museum was being closed instead of moved. Fortunately, she seems to be happy with the new location because once the move was complete, things quieted down again. Maybe Eugenia is now spending her time making more quilts—ghostly quilts that is...

RIVERDALE ROAD

Riverdale Road is an eleven-mile stretch of winding road that runs between Denver's northern suburbs of Thornton and Brighton. The road is paved, but there are no street lights along it, making rainy or snowy nights extra dark and unpredictable.

This road is said to be haunted by various types of entities, including talking animals, demons, a phantom jogger, a lost pioneer wagon family, and a ghostly lady that drifts down the road. Free-floating balls of light, known as orbs, are said to appear floating in front of cars or on the roadside, and a phantom police car patrols the road but disappears when noticed. Some say it cruises there to catch the ghost hotrodders who are known to race this stretch in the dead of night.

Many drivers report feeling unsafe when they drive on Riverdale Road, even in broad daylight. Would you take that drive? If you're brave enough, don't pick up any hitchhikers!

Colorado State Capitol

CHAPTER 4

Denver

Denver was founded in 1858 in an area that was part of the Kansas Territory. The summer of that year, William Green Russell and a group of gold prospectors from Georgia set up a camp on the South Platte River, near the mouth of Cherry Creek.

Across the river there was a group of miners and settlers who had named their settlement St. Charles. A land speculator (someone who buys land in undeveloped areas hoping for a building boom), General William Larimer, managed to join the two groups from opposite sides of the river. He named the combined settlement Denver in honor of the Kansas territorial governor James W. Denver.

Today, Denver is the largest city in the state of Colorado and its state capital. The city has a fascinating history, and lots of people have come and gone, but some have never left...

The Governor's Mansion
(400 East Eighth Avenue)

The Governor's Mansion has traditionally been the home for Colorado's governors while they were in office. Good thing it's pretty big, as they're likely to have company.

One resident spirit is a young woman in a stunning dress, who may have died after she slipped and fell down the stairs in the mansion.

Legend doesn't say why she was dressed so beautifully, but it must have been a special occasion. Was she headed to a party where she planned to dance the night away, but never got the chance? Perhaps that's why she woke up a state trooper who was staying in the mansion one night and demanded that he dance with her. She disappeared soon after, so we'll never know what her plans were if he had refused. She may decide to demand a dance from someone else someday, so wear your dancing shoes if you go to the Governor's Mansion, just in case you have to dance—for your life!

The Peabody-Whitehead Mansion
(1128 Grant Street)

This mansion is said to be home to twelve different spirits, including a young woman named Eloise or Ella, a crying baby, and a waitress who hanged herself in the basement.

The smell of cherry tobacco is often found in the first-floor women's bathroom. Lights flicker, including a chandelier that isn't even connected to electricity. Phones and service bells ring despite being disconnected. There is a whole lot of spooky stuff going on!

The building rents out office space to a few different businesses, and there may be at least one ghost who wants a job. The business-minded spirit leaves numbers on calculators, and stacks of paperwork are often messed up. Fortunately, this "helpful" spirit hasn't demanded a paycheck—yet.

Oscar's House
(1460 Clayton Street, Denver)

A man named Oscar is believed to haunt this house. People say he is still furious about being hanged by construction workers who were upset with his business practices. He's been causing problems for workers at the location ever since. He enjoys misplacing tools they need for their job, and once he even spilled a bucket of paint while the workmen were away from the jobsite. He left the outline of a body in the dried puddle. Talk about holding a grudge!

Stoiberhof
(1022 Humboldt Street, Denver)

This house is haunted by several ghosts, including the original owner, Lena Stoiber, and a sobbing woman holding her own skull. (Gulp!) When Lena's second husband, Hugh Rood, died on the *Titanic*, she refused to believe it. She insisted he was just hiding from her. When she died a few decades later, she left her estate to her seven dogs and the housekeeper. If Hugh came out of hiding, he wasn't going to get a dime from her. He should probably just stay in hiding!

Firehouse No. 1 or Station 1, now the Firefighters' Museum
(1326 Tremont Place, Denver)

This fire station was built in 1909, and it responded to over four hundred fires a year. It was decommissioned in 1975 and underwent several years of renovation before it reopened as a museum dedicated to the history of Denver firefighting.

The ghosts who haunt it enjoy messing with the electrical systems and the computers. Lights turn on and off, and music channels change or turn off completely. Museum staff members say it happens so often, it doesn't even freak them out anymore. Items also move throughout the rooms, including books, a storage bin, and an office chair.

Dark shadows appear and disappear as soon as they are noticed. The sensation of someone watching a visitor or lightly brushing against them have been reported, and orbs have been seen. A favorite spot for paranormal activity is the upstairs men's bathroom, where toilets randomly flush on their own and faucets turn on and off.

The Colorado State Capitol
(200 East Colfax, Denver)

The capitol was opened in November 1894. There are beautiful statues and paintings throughout the building. But there are otherworldly things to be seen as well.

A woman wearing a long dress wanders the halls at night. Late-night workers and maintenance staff often see her gliding quietly in the hallways and down the stairs. She appears to be looking for something, maybe something left in one of the vaults that was used when the building also housed the state treasury.

Other popular ghosts are two disembodied heads seen now and then floating around the basement. No big deal, just a couple of heads with no bodies attached to them. It is believed the heads belonged to two of the "Bloody Espinosas."

Supposedly, the Espinosas committed murders and robberies in 1863 as revenge after some of their family members were attacked and killed by soldiers. They are credited with thirty-two murders in all and even threatened to murder the governor if he didn't restore a five-thousand-acre land grant to their family.

The threat frightened Governor Evans so much he called in the US Cavalry for protection. The military help wasn't needed, though. In October 1863, a man named Tom Tobin walked into Fort Garland with two heads in a sack—the heads of the leaders of the Bloody Espinosas.

The story goes that the heads were then pickled in jars and presented to Governor Evans, who kept them somewhere near his office. The heads were passed to down to future governors until someone ultimately decided it would best to hide them in the basement.

There are no actual heads in jars in the basement today. They were hidden elsewhere at some point, but that doesn't stop them from coming back whenever they please.

Blake Street Vault
(1526 Blake Street, Denver)
Note: The Blake Street Vault is now operating under a new name.

This restaurant is named for a walk-in locker down in the basement of this old building. The locker, or vault, connects to the tunnels that were used to deliver coal to the surrounding neighborhoods. Like the tunnels in other cities, some people say these may have also connected to saloons and other places as well.

The Blake Street Vault has a resident ghost named Lydia. She is also known as "the brown ghost" and "the lady in red." Lydia most likely worked at the saloon, but no one knows exactly when she lived. Both staff and customers have heard Lydia pacing the wooden floors in high heels and have seen her walking downstairs to the basement, where, supposedly, she was murdered.

Her favorite area is the bar. She knocks mugs out of their cubbyholes and likes to twirl pens kept on the counter. When she needs to rest her feet, Lydia prefers one particular booth, third from the right.

If you see her, keep your head down and beware of flying mugs!

The Oxford Hotel
(1600 Seventeenth Street, Denver)

Opened in 1891, the Oxford is Denver's oldest existing boutique hotel. The Cruise Room bar opened in the hotel in 1933, and a ghostly postman appears there from time to time. He has even been heard muttering about needing to deliver gifts to the children. Legend claims this man's body was found on his route, covered with packages he didn't get to deliver before he died.

But the mail carrier doesn't bother anyone in the bar, unlike the hotel's resident spirit, Florence Montague. This ghost inhabits room 320 and is known to yank the covers off sleeping guests, especially young men. And sometimes she pinches them on their arms, too. Her message is clear: "Get out of my room, young man!" So remember, room 320 belongs to Florence. Sleep there (or try to) if you dare.

The Hotel Teatro
(1100 Fourteenth Street, Denver)

This location was originally the Denver Tramway Building, opened in 1911. It has had several owners, including the University of Colorado.

The Hotel Teatro opened there in 1997, along with its restaurant, the Nickel. If you stand in the lobby waiting for a table, there's a good chance you will experience some paranormal activity, including ghost sightings and random lights that appear out of nowhere.

Be on the lookout for "Tool Man," a former mechanic who can be spotted walking down the hallway still carrying his tools. You might think he's real until he vanishes into thin air. Staff members think he may have died at work and is now trapped at the hotel.

Strange red lights sometimes shine from under an elevator door, as well as from under a guest room door. The red light is accompanied by whispering voices. Both the light and the voices quickly disappear when anyone tries to track down their source. There were apartments on the top floors in the 1940s, and one woman who owned a unit on the eighth floor refused to leave when the owners told her they were selling the building. She barricaded herself inside her apartment, and not long after, her family discovered her dead body in the building's basement. The family sold her apartment, but some people believe she is still there, still refusing to leave.

The Mayan Theatre
(110 Broadway, Denver)

This gorgeous theater opened in 1930, but by the 1960s, it was looking old and run down. It was nearly demolished in 1985, but new owners reopened it in 1986 with three movie screens and a full restaurant.

Many original features of the theater have been removed, but some guests may have stayed in their seats, the hallways, and the screening rooms. The lights flicker at odd times, and janitors have seen a ghostly figure wandering around the place. This figure also shows up and stares at staffers while they work. If you go, you might catch a double-feature: a movie and a ghost!

Denver Public Library
(10 West Fourteenth Avenue Parkway, Denver)

Imagine one day you go to the Denver Public Library, looking for a book. But instead of finding your next good read, you find a disgruntled ghost! The library opened in 1910 in a much smaller building—so small, in fact, that three-quarters of the library's materials had to be stored in the basement. Library staff soon realized there was an unhappy spirit down there who had no interest in sharing the basement with all those books. Sometimes it would shove employees when they came downstairs. One security guard was so frightened by it that he quit his job on the spot.

But maybe it wasn't the books the unfriendly ghost had a problem with after all.

When the library moved its collection to its current location, the entity seems to have moved right along with it! And it might still prefer the lowest floor. The staff at the current location will only venture downstairs in pairs.

Maybe the ghost simply doesn't like to have its reading time interrupted. It would take a long time to read a whole basement full of books, and how's a ghost supposed to plan what to read next if people keep rearranging the stacks?

Tivoli Student Union
(900 Auraria Parkway, Denver)

This was originally one of twelve buildings used by the Tivoli Brewery, constructed in 1866. Some of the brewery equipment is still there. In 1994, the Tivoli became the student union for three different universities: Community College of Denver, Metropolitan State College (Metro), and the University of Colorado (CU). But it isn't just students who meet up here.

Many of the building's echoes are thought to be from past students who have studied and met with friends there. Voices and whispers echo throughout the building, along with noises coming from the third floor that sound as if an elegant party is taking place. The party noise drifts through the vents, but stops immediately if anyone tries to investigate. Stop crashing the ghost party, you nosy humans!

The Generous Ghost on Ellsworth Avenue

Imagine you are having dinner with friends and you lose track of time, laughing and talking. You glance at your phone and realize your parking meter is about to run out, so you tell your friends you'll be right back. You've parked on Ellsworth Avenue, one of the streets where the city put in a bunch of parking meters in the 1990s and early 2000s. You run down Ellsworth Avenue, hoping to beat the meter. If you're too late, and the parking meter has expired, chances are you will have gotten a nice big parking ticket. Unless someone unexpectedly helped you out. (And back in the 1990s, there had been reports of someone—or something—plunking coins into the parking meters along Ellsworth Avenue.)

As you approach your car, you see someone, or a portion of someone. You can see right through him! And he's stopped dead in front of your car. What is he doing? Is he dangerous? Then he reaches into his pocket... oh, no, what is he going to pull out? You slow down to assess the situation from a safe distance.

Wait, is this see-through guy putting coins into your meter? It is. A ghost just bought you more time! Since it's pretty much impossible to repay a ghost, maybe you can pay it forward instead and drop some coins into someone else's nearly expired meter someday.

Highlands Ranch Mansion

CHAPTER 5

Leadville

Horace Tabor trudged into Colorado in 1859, looking to strike it rich with gold. For years, he and his wife, Augusta, patiently worked and saved their pennies. Their goal was to invest in a successful gold mine. In 1878, it finally happened—a mine he grubstaked (invested in) hit it big, and so did Horace and Augusta.

Augusta remained budget-minded, but Horace wanted to live more lavishly. He didn't want to worry about money anymore. He divorced Augusta and married a woman named Elizabeth, known as "Baby Doe." Horace and Baby Doe enjoyed an extravagant lifestyle until the Panic of 1893, when the United States was struck by the worst economic crisis it had ever experienced.

Horace's money ran out, and he had to take a job as Denver's postmaster, a position he held until he died in April 1899. Baby Doe lived on, in a shack and in poverty, until her death in 1935.

Horace and Baby Doe had owned several homes, and all of them were eventually destroyed. Her brother Peter McCourt had a palatial home built in 1888 at 555 East Eighth Avenue in Denver. Horace, Baby Doe, and their daughters lived there with Peter for a few years after they lost all their money. Witnesses say Horace continues to show up in the house, not in his postmaster uniform, but in a top hat and tails, dressed like a rich man ready for a night on the town or a fancy party.

Baby Doe's shack still stands and is now a museum near Leadville. Its caretaker assured a reporter that Baby Doe is still around. She especially enjoys her rocking chair. Visitors have been shocked to find her already occupying it when they tried to sit down. And photos of Baby Doe and Augusta were displayed next to one another for a while, but they were mysteriously moved around. Lights in the museum go on and off even after lightbulbs are unscrewed.

Horace and Baby Doe are also thought to still visit their favorite entertainment spot in Leadville, the Tabor Opera House (308 Harrison Avenue, Leadville), which Horace founded and built. He has been seen on the stage and in the audience. Ghosts don't need season tickets—they have infinity tickets and can show up anytime and anywhere they please.

LITTLETON

One of the reasons this Denver suburb was founded was the need for water. Lots of people in search of gold moved to the area in 1859, and that meant that merchants and farmers were needed to provide supplies and food for the gold miners.

Irrigation ditches were needed to carry water to those stores and farms. One of the men who was hired to design the irrigation system was Richard Sullivan Little. He was a young engineer from New Hampshire. He brought his wife, Angeline, and they became the first two residents of Littleton.

The town has grown and changed a lot since then, but the downtown area is in the National Register of Historic places, which helps to protect and preserve historic buildings. And where old buildings remain, so do old spirits.

Main Street in Littleton is home to quite a bit of ghostly action.

Littleton Town Hall Arts Center
(2450 West Main, Littleton)

Built in the 1920s, this building has been home to all sorts of official departments, including the city offices, a jail, and the volunteer fire department. The ghosts here must have a great time because their laughter and music can be heard late into the night. Only occasionally does anyone hear banging on the walls, but that grumpy party-pooper doesn't keep the rest of the spirits quiet for long. Unlike some ghosts in other places, who calm down as soon as they are discovered, the party here never ends, not for long, anyway.

Littleton Cemetery
(6155 South Prince Street, Littleton)

Someone famous is buried here. But he wasn't a gold miner who struck it rich, a movie star, a politician, or an important businessman. So who is he?

A cannibal! (A cannibal is somebody who eats human flesh.) Alferd Packer is famous for being the "the Colorado Cannibal," and this is where his body was laid to rest, along with his pet goat. (The story goes that Packer was traveling through the mountains during a harsh winter with a group of prospectors. Packer claimed that four of the men had died naturally from the extreme winter conditions and the starving survivors ate them. When only Packer and one other man, Shannon Bell, remained alive, Bell went insane and threatened to kill Packer. Packer said he shot Bell in self-defense and eventually ate his corpse.)

Maybe *infamous* is a better word for Alfred Packer. He and his goat are said to haunt the cemetery. Stay on the lookout for orbs and other floating things. And make sure you've washed off the smell of your last meal.

The Highlands Ranch Mansion
(9950 East Gateway Drive, Littleton)

The Highlands Ranch Mansion is open for free tours, public events, and rentals. But many visitors report sensing a feeling of isolation or sadness during their visit, probably connected to the ghost of a young girl that is often spotted there. She is thought to be Julia, the daughter of Frank Kistler, who bought the mansion in 1926. The property was known as the Diamond K ranch during his ownership, and he raised dairy cattle and livestock for breeding.

Frank Kistler remarried when Julia was young, and her new stepmom came with sons.

It is said that Frank neglected Julia and paid more attention to his new family. He would take his stepsons out while Julia was left behind to watch from her upstairs bedroom window. Her ghost is seen looking out that window and the west bedroom window. She has also been spotted walking in the upstairs hallways.

Visitors have also heard sobs, and the clock in the great hall continued to chime even after it had been broken for years. Frank Kistler was forced to sell the mansion during the Great Depression in the 1930s because he could no longer afford it. But it seems Julia may still be waiting for her father to come back, pay attention to her, and no longer leave her behind.

CASTLE ROCK

Pioneers on expeditions in the 1850s couldn't help but notice the large slab of rock sitting high on one of the buttes dotting this area of the Front Range, and they called it Castle Rock. There are other formations in Colorado also named Castle Rock, including one in Golden and one in Boulder Canyon, but this one became a landmark along the migrant trail to Denver.

In 1872, Silas Madge began mining rhyolite lava rock from the tops of local buttes. Builders found rhyolite easy to work with and a number of Castle Rock's historic buildings were constructed from it, including the courthouse and the Castle Rock Depot. The rock was even used for the Windsor Hotel in Denver.

Legend says the nearby town of Franktown was originally supposed to be the seat of

Douglas County. But residents of Castle Rock didn't agree with that. So they sneaked over in the dead of night and changed all the records. However it happened, Castle Rock—not Franktown—became the county seat in 1874 and an official city in 1881. The recognizable rock formation that gave it its name is still clearly visible today. And if you keep your eyes open, you might see some of the area's original citizens, maybe even some of the ones who pulled that late-night prank with the county records.

Stumpy's Pizza
(138 South Wilcox Street, Castle Rock)

Pots and pans are put away every night at closing time at Stumpy's Pizza, but they are frequently found scattered all over the kitchen when the first employee arrives the next day. Sometimes flour has been spilled onto the floor, and tiny child-sized footprints can be seen in it. Sounds like some young ghosts are hungry for pizza and can't wait for the place to reopen. It's hard to make pizza without making a little bit of a mess. And who wants to clean up once you've finished eating? Plus, it's hard to force ghosts to tidy up after their pizza party.

Old Stone Church
(210 Third Street, Castle Rock)

This building got its start in 1887 as the St. Francis of Assisi Catholic Church. After the congregation moved, it eventually became a restaurant in 1975. It's now Scileppi's at the Old Stone Church, and the haunted eatery is home to several apparitions.

They can be seen frequently on the second floor in what was the original choir loft. The most popular ghost is a little girl dressed in white. One young boy described her as having "something wrong with the back of her head."

The reflection of a woman standing on the main staircase has been seen in a mirror. A manager who saw her reflection said he had to walk through "a thick wall of clammy air" to move past this ghost.

Sugar packet holders fly through the air, chairs move, lights turn on and off on their own, and pans and utensils have fallen off hooks and shelves in the kitchen. It seems like Scileppi's might have a phantom staff working right alongside the living staff. The ghosts probably think they are a big help, but the living staff probably think otherwise.

DC. Oakes High School
(961 Plum Creek Boulevard, Castle Rock)

This location originally housed the Philip S. Miller Library. Jamie LaRue, the director of the

Douglas County Libraries, had an unsettling experience there on a Sunday morning in 1992. The library was closed, but LaRue saw movement out of the corner of his eye. He turned to see a tall man with long hair, dressed in buckskin with fringe, walking through the lobby toward the restroom. LaRue went out to the lobby to see who was there, but he couldn't find the man.

The restrooms were empty, and all the doors to the library were still locked. Could the apparition have been connected to the Arapahoe and Cheyenne Indians who still roamed the area when settlers moved in during the 1870s? Perhaps he had gotten lost, or maybe he was traveling one of the Indian paths in the area and this pesky building was in his way. Native Americans were using those trails long before the library showed up, so why should he have to go around it?

Chamber of Commerce
(420 Jerry Street, Castle Rock)

This stone building was originally a house, and at one point, it was owned by Victoria Anderson Honnold, who inherited it from her parents. Victoria died on December 9, 1942, and was buried between her first and second husbands in the Cedar Hill Cemetery. It is rumored that Victoria considered herself a prominent socialite, and it seems life after death out on Cedar Hill is too quiet for her.

Victoria prefers her former home on Jerry Street, and she makes her return known with noises like snoring and a buzzing sound that comes from an upstairs bathroom. Doors swing open on their own, and she may be obsessed with the telephone. Staffers often answer the ringing phone to find no one on the other end. Maybe Victoria is trying to call other socialites to inform them of her next party or to ask them to join a committee or make a donation to a charity. An important lady's work is never done.

The Castle Rock Museum
(420 Elbert Street, Castle Rock)

The Castle Rock Museum is said to be one of the town's most active buildings when it comes to paranormal happenings. It began as a small train depot on Third Street. The Denver & Rio Grande Railroad ran between Denver and Colorado City (now known as Colorado Springs) and was completed in 1871. In 1874, Castle Rock was granted a depot.

The depot was moved from its original location near the train tracks to its current location in 1970. It was a slow process, but the Castle Rock Historical Society wanted to preserve the building. It became a museum in 1996.

Some ghostly travelers still treat the space

like a depot, particularly around the preserved ticket window and baggage area. A paranormal investigation captured several EVPs, including one that seems to say, "tickets," along with various whispers and sounds of movement. (You remember EVPs, right? Electronic voice phenomena, thought to be the voices of ghosts captured in a recording.)

Much of the activity happens around the stationmaster's uniform that is kept on display. The uniform belonged to E.G. Breselow, who was the Rio Grande station agent for almost fifty years. He retired around the same time the railroad closed its regular stop in Castle Rock. Maybe he figures if this is where his uniform hangs, he should hang around, too.

Red Rocks Amphitheater

CHAPTER 6

Larkspur

This small town, named for the many larkspur flowers growing in the area, began with a post office in 1871. Today, Larkspur is known for the large renaissance festival it hosts every summer. It's a rowdy event with jousting, wild animals, a daily royal parade, and a comedy pair called "Puke and Snot," and it attracts thousands of visitors.

Spur of the Moment
(8885 Spruce Mountain Road, Larkspur)

One character in town who definitely isn't there for the Renaissance Festival is believed to be the spirit of local rancher Fred White. White died in 1993 at the age of seventy-four. He prefers to be entertained at the Spur of the Moment restaurant and bar.

After a long hard day on the ranch, what cowboy could resist the smell of burgers sizzling on the grill or so many customers having such a good time? The ghost wears a bandana and a dark hat similar to White's. He began showing up not long after the building was renovated and reopened in 1995.

A bartender was the first to see him, and she described him as being in his forties, with bright eyes and a weathered face, wearing jeans and cowboy boots. He smiled at her and then disappeared. Later, when she was telling someone at the bar about the ghost, a ten-gallon bucket suddenly flipped over. How nice to have the ghost confirm her story!

A cook was the second to spot him, leaning against a wall. The cook thought he was an early customer and, despite knowing the door was locked, rushed over to seat him. But the cowboy vanished before the cook reached him.

The ghost appears younger than Fred White was at the time of his death, but he seems to have the same caring nature Fred was known to have. He does, however, enjoy creating a little mischief now and then. Don't expect the television to stay on the same channel or at the same volume if he is around. He also likes to move the barstools, and he might pull your ponytail, especially if you are a man.

The employees like Fred White. They say he is their protector. He often keeps them company until closing time and will even turn the lights off for them at the end of the night. Who needs a security guard when you have a ghost on the job?

NATURAL WONDERS WITH UNNATURAL OCCURENCES

Red Rocks Park and Amphitheater
(18300 West Alameda Parkway, Morrison)

This 868-acre park features a world-famous natural amphitheater. An amphitheater is an open circular structure with a round space in the center bordered by tiered rows of seating for spectators. In other words, it's an outdoor auditorium. This one gets its name from the large brownish-red rock formations that surround it.

The rocks provide near-flawless acoustics, which makes Red Rocks a great place for musicians to perform. And hundreds of bands and singers from around the world have performed here to sold out crowds. The ghosts who haunt this popular concert venue, however, are not as well known.

A bearded old miner wearing a dirty brown hat and holding a bottle is the ghost seen most often. He is said to appear on the restricted side of the railing. He looks around for a moment or two and then disappears.

There is another ghost who is much more frightening: a headless woman riding horseback, holding a bloody hatchet! No word if it's the same hatchet that chopped off her head or if she chopped off someone else's head as payback. The staff claim she is there to protect Red Rocks from troublemakers. They don't say what the punishment will be if she catches anybody causing problems. But that bloody hatchet is a good clue.

Castlewood Canyon
(entrances on both Highway 86, east of Franktown, and Highway 83, south of Franktown)

This state park contains what's left of Castlewood Canyon Dam, which burst in 1933 after intense rains, sending a fifteen-foot wall of water as far as Denver (over thirty miles away!). The dam was never rebuilt.

Camping overnight isn't allowed here, but the park offers great trails for hiking and climbing. The natural beauty and outdoor adventure opportunities of Castlewood Canyon are probably why some visitors are reluctant to ever leave, particularly one young man who lost his life there.

The murdered body of twenty-six-year-old Roger Floth was found under the canyon's arched bridge on April 7, 1965. Although police had two suspects at the time, no one was prosecuted for the crime. Now the many strange noises, odd events, and misplaced items at the visitors' center are all attributed to Floth. The center's radio sometimes turns itself on and off. Strange banging can be heard on the outside wall, like a fist is beating on it. And on the anniversary of the discovery of his body, a rack of postcards fell over in center as if it had been deliberately shoved. Sounds to me like it's Roger Floth making himself known.

On at least one occasion, he may have been trying to communicate something important through his actions. One evening, the back door of the visitors' center slammed harder than usual. When a staffer went to investigate, he found three books on the floor. One was from a shelf all the way across the room, and it had landed "upright and open." The page it was opened to mentioned some equipment that had been removed from the mechanical room years earlier. The staff member thought it could have been Floth trying to get them to check something in the mechanical room, but he didn't follow up on it.

A few weeks later, a defective water filter in the mechanical room failed, and the visitors' center was flooded with six-inches of water. The staffer said, "If only we'd listened to Roger."

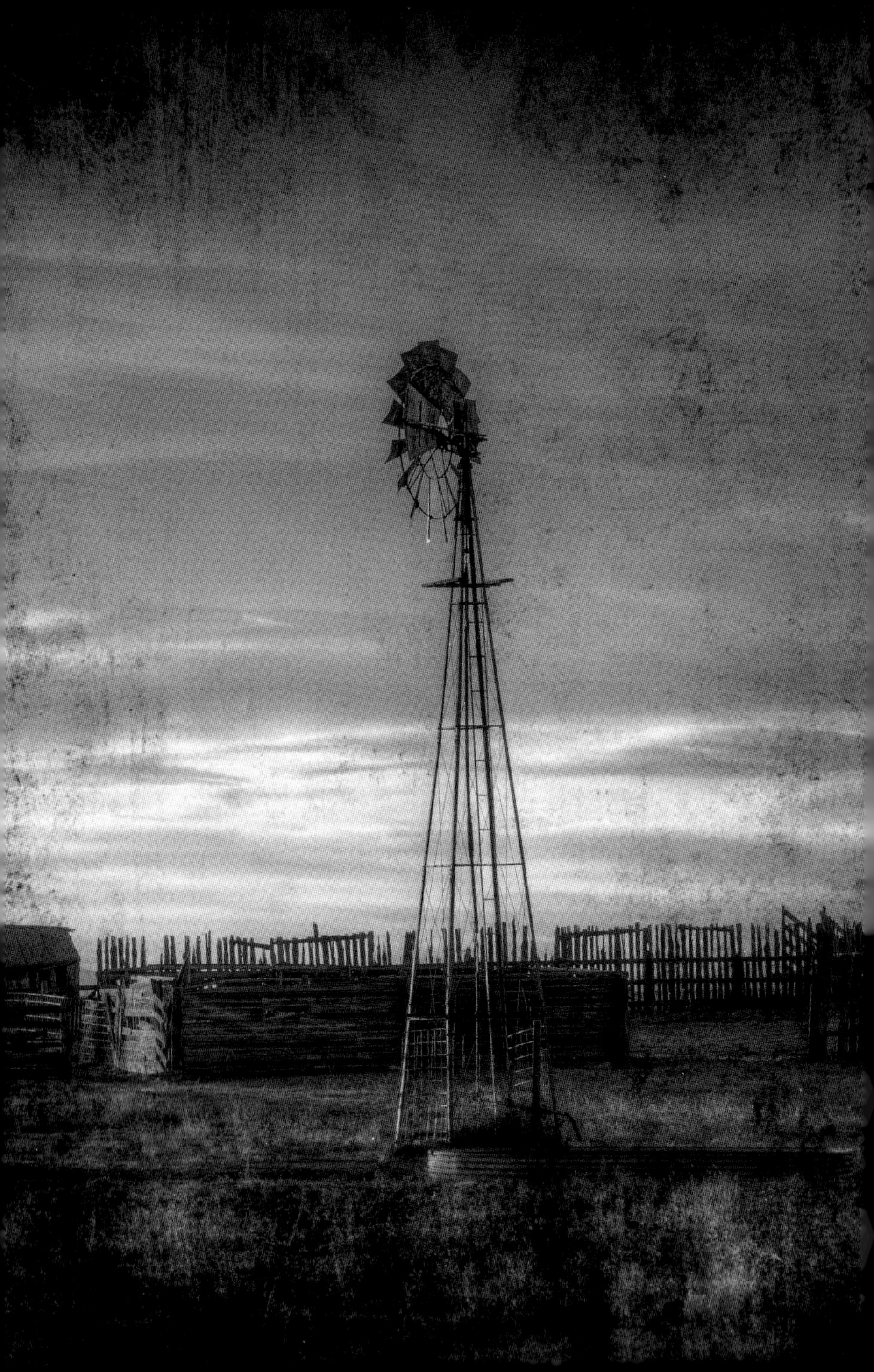

CHAPTER 7

Colorado Springs

Colorado Springs, established in 1859, was first known as Colorado City. It started as a supply camp. Freight wagons came from north and south to access the Santa Fe Trail. Native peoples passed through on their way to hunting grounds or the healing waters nearby. Farmers and ranchers came into town for groceries and some recreation. And the many miners who came to the area because of the Pikes

Peak goldrush came down from the mountains for supplies. A lot of people passed through Colorado City.

General William Jackson Palmer knew putting a railroad route through the area would be a smart idea, but his employer, the Kansas Pacific Railway, did not agree. This led General Palmer to start his own railroad, the Denver & Rio Grande Railroad, in 1870. His railroad reached Colorado City in 1871. Close by, he had founded Fountain City, and eventually, Colorado City and Fountain City were combined to form what would become Colorado Springs.

Penrose-St. Francis Health Services Center
(2222 North Nevada Avenue, Colorado Springs)

Penrose-St. Francis is a Catholic-based hospital, and at least one nun from long ago refuses to leave. She wanders the hallways with blood on her habit. Whose blood is on her clothing? We may never know. She doesn't seem to want to explain herself. This nun is still busy doing her good work. She has no time to stop and talk.

THE PIONEERS MUSEUM
(215 South Tejon Street, Colorado Springs)

In 1903, the museum was the El Paso County Courthouse. Many people walked through the doors of that courthouse, including captured outlaws and the judges who would decide their punishments. Today, museum visitors come to see the pioneer exhibits and maybe, if they're lucky, catch a glimpse of the building's very own guardian spirit.

The ghost is a former manager who was killed during an argument with a staff member over his pay. This managing ghost patrols the halls, making sure things are done properly, and then he goes home to his old apartment in the building, where he doesn't have to argue with anybody about their paycheck. He gets a good rest, and then he makes his rounds through the museum again.

Harrison High School
(2755 Janitell Road, Colorado Springs)

The auditorium at this high school is home to a spirit named Malcolm. He is a former student, and he's a pretty noble guy. A young woman once slipped on the catwalk and nearly fell, but someone caught her and pulled her back to safety. When she turned to thank her hero, she found no one there, but she felt a soft kiss on her cheek. What a romantic ghost!

The Antlers Hotel
(4 South Cascade Avenue, Colorado Springs)

Some hotels have been the sites of bloody murders and terrible accidents, and as a result, troubled spirits roam their halls in search of peace or revenge. But the Antlers Hotel is haunted by much happier ghosts.

A woman dressed in a long evening gown can be seen coming down the back stairs. She's obviously headed to a fancy party, and she has no interest in upsetting anyone on her way out. The elegant lady seems to be looking forward to her night. A young girl appears in some of the guest rooms, but she doesn't cause any trouble (like some kids do). And a male figure often quietly sips his drink at Judge Baldwin's Bar. This was likely a spot he enjoyed during his life, and he's still enjoying it in his afterlife. When that bar says, "We serve spirits," they really mean it!

The Broadmoor Hotel
(1 Lake Avenue, Colorado Springs)

The Broadmoor Hotel, nicknamed "the Grand Dame of the Rockies," was originally opened in 1891 as the Broadmoor Casino. Its first owner was a Prussian count whose last name was Pourtales. Spencer Penrose and his wife, Julie, bought the casino in 1916 and spent two million dollars renovating it. In 1918, it reopened as the most elegant hotel in the area and has never been completely closed. Some sections have been closed for repairs over the years, but never the entire hotel.

Like so many other buildings in Colorado, the Broadmoor sits on a set of tunnels. Between the 779 rooms in the hotel and the tunnels that run under it, there is plenty of room for ghosts to make their home here.

Staffers notice one spirit on a regular basis. She is a woman dressed in 1920s-style clothes, and she roams the main section of the Broadmoor at night. It might be Julie Penrose, keeping watch over her beautiful hotel, or it could be the Countess Pourtales, checking in on her husband's former property. Either way, there is a ghostly woman keeping an eye on things at the Broadmoor.

PUEBLO

Pueblo is located right where the Arkansas River meets Fountain Creek. At one time, the Arkansas River marked the borderline between Mexico and the United States. During its existence, Pueblo has had the flags of several different countries flying over it.

When the Pikes Peak rush began in 1859, El Pueblo, as it was known at the time, was a supply fort that serviced travelers and miners heading north and west. The railroad arrived in 1872 and added to the city's growth and progress. Colorado Fuel and Iron (CF&I) was the major employer in town for nearly a century, leading to the nickname of "Steel City." Pueblo was also known for being the saddle-making capital of the world.

Pueblo was a diverse place right from the start. Work at CF&I was hot, dirty, and dangerous, but the mill didn't require workers to be able to speak English. This drew immigrant workers from all over. At one point, over forty languages were spoken in the mill, and two dozen foreign-language newspapers were published in town. Residents of Pueblo today possess vast and varied heritage. Many are descendants of original settlers. And some of their ancestors still show up around town.

The Damon Runyon Repertory Theater
(611 North Main Street, Pueblo)

Three spirits haunt this theater together: an aggressive man, a woman who seems to be the protector of the group, and a little girl. The little girl used to insist on keeping all the lights burning downstairs until a permanent nightlight was installed. At least once, a radio kept surfing through channels even though it was turned off, unplugged, and had no batteries. When a man picked it up to investigate the sounds, the radio went silent. Pictures sometimes fly off the walls in the theater, and doors open by themselves. During the production of every other play or so, lights will flip on and off, and cue cards will disappear. Obviously, these ghosts think they are theater critics!

Pueblo Fire Museum
(116 Broadway Avenue, Pueblo)

At least one spirit here likes to drive the firetrucks. Yes, you read that right. Maybe it's someone who was a firefighter before they died, or maybe they always wanted to be one. Either way, they frequently manage to turn on several of the trucks, and once, a truck not only started, but drove itself around the block before parking and turning itself back off! An apparition has also been spotted sitting in one of the trucks. People passing by the building report hearing engines running and vehicles moving around inside the building at night. So far, this ghost has an excellent driving record—not a single accident!

A GHOSTLY TELEGRAM

In the mid-1800s, signs of modernization and progress sprung up along the trails through the Front Range in the form of telegraph poles. This new, easier means of communication was the beginning of the end for the Pony Express. (The Pony Express delivered mail quickly across the western United States. Men on small, fast horses would ride segments of the trail to carry mail between Missouri and California. The service lasted for only about a year and a half in the early 1860s.)

With telegraphs, communication throughout Colorado and the entire West would be much faster and more effective. By late 1861, the overland telegraph had expanded across the whole country, connecting America's West Coast to the East Coast.

But in 1891, the *Rocky Mountain News* printed one of the most mysterious telegraph stories ever recorded. The Denver telegraph office ("D") was contacted repeatedly by "AZ," claiming a full message would be provided only when they were ready to receive it. When the full message finally arrived, it came in too quickly for anyone at the Denver office to translate the code. The sender signed his name as "KX"—a mystery since there was no employee or office known as AZ or KX.

The garbled message repeated itself night after night. KX eventually explained how to decipher it, and the decoded message read as follows: "I was a man who in my time on earth drank considerable and one night was killed on what is known as the continental ridgeway or divide. Until this message is deciphered I will not rest easy in my grave R.D. Haskall." The night chief operator clicked back, "Don't 13," which means "Don't understand."

Quickly, the sound rattled back on, and in Morse code, another message explained that Haskall was "killed on the old Pueblo trail, a few miles from what is now Palmer Lake on the Continental Divide. My spirit has roamed about and. . . . I cannot rest in my grave. The telegraph pole from which I am sending this is planted directly over my grave. . . . I will call you up regularly for three nights, and if I raise you, answer."

Two of the operators in the Denver office went out to search for this pole, which Haskall claimed was fifteen miles from the lake. They found it—right where he said it was! As they sat there, wondering what to do next, a dim blue light appeared, followed by the white shape of a man holding a telegraph key. The apparition climbed the pole, cut the wires, sent a telegraph, slid back down the pole, and disappeared.

When the operators returned to the Denver office, they read the message he had sent: "Your two investigators are here. They have seen me. Farewell to earth. I have been heard and seen. I am satisfied. Good-bye, H."

Message received, H. Safe travels.

Well, that's the end of our tour. You've traveled down the full length of the Front Range from north to south and met quite a few of its ghosts. There are more, of course. Colorado's Front Range is the perfect place to learn about history, experience the great outdoors, and maybe even meet a few spirits.

What are you waiting for? Get to exploring on your own!

Shelli Timmons writes for kids of all ages. After many years working with numbers, she realized she liked letters a whole lot more, so she stepped away from the world of finance and entered the realm of stories. She loves old houses and buildings, and is always open to sharing space with a ghost or two. She currently lives in Central Texas in a house much newer than she'd prefer, with an equal number of people and dogs.

Check out some of the other Spooky America titles available now!

Spooky America was adapted from the creeptastic Haunted America series, for adults. Haunted America explores historical haunts in cities and regions across America. Each book chronicles both the widely known and less-familiar history behind local ghosts and other unexplained mysteries. Here's more from the original *Ghosts & Legends of Colorado's Front Range* author Cindy Brick: